PRAYING WITH
MOTHER ANGELICA

PRAYING WITH MOTHER ANGELICA

*Meditations on the Rosary,
the Way of the Cross, and Other Prayers*

EWTN PUBLISHING, INC.
Irondale, Alabama

Cover and interior design by Perceptions Design Studio.

Cover art: detail from official portrait by John Howard Sanden.
Interior art: courtesy of CCWATERSHED.ORG.

Biblical references in this book are taken from Jerusalem Bible, © 1966 by Darton Longman and Todd Ltd and Doubleday and Company Ltd., with the exception of those in the section on the Luminous Mysteries, which are taken from the New Jerusalem Bible, © 1985 by Darton Longman & Todd Ltd and Doubleday and Company Ltd.

EWTN Publishing, Inc.
5817 Old Leeds Road, Irondale, AL 35210
Distributed by Sophia Institute Press, Box 5284, Manchester, NH 03108

Library of Congress Cataloging-in-Publication Data
Names: M. Angelica (Mary Angelica), Mother, 1923-
Title: Praying with Mother Angelica : meditations on the Rosary, the Way of the Cross, and Other Prayers.
Description: Irondale, Alabama : EWTN Pub., Inc., [2016] | Mini-books My Life in the Rosary, Living Way of the Cross, Ad Lib With the Lord, copyright 1976, Our Lady of the Angels Monastery, 3222 County Road 548, Hanceville, Alabama 35077, www.olamshrine.com, and printed with the ecclesiastical approval of Joseph G. Vath, D.D., Bishop of Birmingham, Alabama, USA.
Identifiers: LCCN 2015038433 | ISBN 9781682780008 (hardcover : alk. paper)
Subjects: LCSH: Rosary. | Stations of the Cross.
Classification: LCC BX2163 .M23 2016 | DDC 242/.74—dc23 LC record available at http://lccn.loc.gov/2015038433

CONTENTS

EDITOR'S NOTE

The prayers and meditations reproduced here originally appeared in three mini-books written by Mother Angelica in the 1970s: *My Life in the Rosary*, *Living Way of the Cross*, and *Ad Lib with the Lord*. By the middle of that decade, the Nuns of Our Lady of the Angels Monastery in Irondale, Alabama, had acquired their own printing equipment and were churning out as many as twenty-five thousand copies of these pamphlets and others per day. This was truly a nascent mass-media operation, one that would lead to the creation of EWTN — the Eternal Word Television Network.

We have made one addition to Mother's work for this prayer book. Pope St. John Paul II did not promulgate the Luminous Mysteries until 2002 in his Apostolic Letter *Rosarium Virginis Mariae*, by which time Mother's health had declined such that she could not compose further reflections. The meditations on these Mysteries offered here are inspired by Mother's style and are based on her televised teachings on these five pivotal moments in Jesus' ministry.

MEDITATIONS

—— *on* ——

THE ROSARY

HOW TO PRAY THE ROSARY

Sign of the Cross
Apostles' Creed
Our Father
Three Hail Marys

For each mystery:
Announce the Mystery
Our Father
Ten Hail Marys
Glory Be
Fátima Prayer

Hail Holy Queen
Rosary Prayer
Sign of the Cross

The Prayers of the Rosary

Apostles' Creed

I believe in God, the Father Almighty, Creator of Heaven and earth, and in Jesus Christ, His only Son, Our Lord, who was conceived by the Holy Spirit, born of the Virgin Mary, suffered under Pontius Pilate, was crucified, died, and was buried. He descended into hell; the third day He arose again from the dead; He ascended into Heaven and is seated at the right hand of God, the Father Almighty; from thence He shall come to judge

the living and the dead. I believe in the Holy
Spirit, the holy Catholic Church, the Commu-
nion of Saints, the forgiveness of sins, the resurrection of the body, and life everlasting. Amen.

Our Father

Our Father, who art in Heaven, hallowed be Thy
Name; Thy kingdom come; Thy will be done on
earth as it is in Heaven. Give us this day our daily
bread, and forgive us our trespasses as we forgive
those who trespass against us; and lead us not
into temptation, but deliver us from evil. Amen.

Hail Mary

Hail Mary, full of grace! The Lord is with
thee; blessed art thou among women, and

blessed is the fruit of thy womb, Jesus. Holy
Mary, Mother of God, pray for us sinners
now and at the hour of our death. Amen.

Glory Be

Glory be to the Father, and to the Son, and to the
Holy Spirit. As it was in the beginning, is now,
and ever shall be, world without end. Amen.

Fátima Prayer

O my Jesus, forgive us our sins, save us from the
fires of hell, and lead all souls to Heaven, especially those most in need of Thy mercy.

Hail Holy Queen

Hail, holy Queen, Mother of Mercy, our life, our sweetness, and our hope. To thee do we cry, poor banished children of Eve. To thee do we send up our sighs, mourning, and weeping in this valley of tears. Turn then, O most gracious advocate, thine eyes of mercy toward us; and after this our exile, show unto us the blessed fruit of thy womb, Jesus. O clement! O loving! O sweet Virgin Mary! Pray for us, O holy Mother of God, that we may be made worthy of the promises of Christ.

Rosary Prayer

O God, whose only-begotten Son, by His life,
death, and Resurrection, has purchased for
us the rewards of eternal salvation. Grant,
we beseech Thee, that while meditating on
these mysteries of the most holy Rosary of
the Blessed Virgin Mary, we may both imitate what they contain and obtain what they
promise, through Christ Our Lord. Amen.

Most Sacred Heart of Jesus, have mercy on us.
Immaculate Heart of Mary, pray for us.

The

JOYFUL

MYSTERIES

Prayed on Mondays and Saturdays

First Joyful Mystery

THE ANNUNCIATION

"Hail, full of grace,
the Lord is with thee."

LUKE 1:28

*We pray for a respect
for the sanctity of life: Our Father,
ten Hail Marys, Glory Be.*

Meditation

When the darkness of sin covered mankind, your love and humility, kind Mother, turned the face of the Father toward His erring children. Although the message of the angel was difficult for you to understand, you accepted the will of God with trust and love.

You questioned neither His power nor His wisdom but asked only how this great mystery was to be accomplished. We live in a world that does not accept the Father's wisdom, does not trust in His providence, does not believe in His power. We cannot see beyond tomorrow, and so the present moment is bereft of the knowledge of His presence.

Your trust in the Father's will made the miraculous simple. Why can't we trust His plan in our lives as you trusted Him in yours? Even though the Child born to be the Savior would suffer untold agonies, you never for a moment hesitated in your Fiat. The women of our day fear the future of their unborn children. In an act of misguided zeal they sometimes deprive the Father of the opportunity to manifest His power, bestow upon us His goodness and populate the Kingdom with children of light.

Give us a share of your faith and hope that we may bow before the infinite wisdom of God and accept the treasures He deigns to bestow upon us. Let us leave creation to His omnipotence, the future to His providence, and mankind to His wisdom.

THE VISITATION

"When Elizabeth heard the greeting of
Mary the babe in her womb leapt, and
she was filled with the Holy Spirit."

— LUKE 1:41

*We pray for the elderly and
for respect for all persons: Our Father,
ten Hail Marys, Glory Be.*

Meditation

What impulse of love made you hurry to visit your cousin Elizabeth, kind Mother? At a moment when you had every right to rest in the jubilant news that you would be the Mother of the Messiah, you left the place of your exaltation.

Your compassionate heart turned toward Elizabeth. In her old age, she needed the comfort of your youth. The Child in your womb, conceived by the Holy Spirit, began His work of redemption by sanctifying John.

Your zeal to carry Jesus to others, no matter what the cost, embarrasses us and causes us to blush with shame. We neglect the aged because we are too busy. We permit the generation gap to widen because we do not possess the love to bridge the distance. We permit social injustice because we do not wish to be our brother's keeper.

Holy Mary, bring Jesus to us through the merits of your visit to Elizabeth. Obtain for us the graces we need to magnify the Lord by our humility in dealing with our neighbor, our concern for the aged, our zeal for social justice, and our courage when duty calls for sacrifice.

Third Joyful Mystery

THE NATIVITY

"And she brought forth her first-born Son
and wrapped Him in swaddling clothes."

— LUKE 2:7

We pray for mothers and for the poor:
Our Father, ten Hail Marys, Glory Be.

Meditation

We look with wonder at the wisdom of God as the promised woman gives birth to the promised Messiah in a cold cave! Deprived of all material things, the Splendor of Heaven entered the world—that work of His hands—in abject poverty.

Jesus and Mary want us to know that their love for us is pure and devoid of any selfishness. The Mother of God says to all mothers, "Let the dignity of your motherhood rise above created things and the richness of your love cover your poverty."

Can we ever imagine the ecstasy of Mary as her eyes met the eyes of God in her tiny infant? Can our hearts ever feel the agony as she saw His outstretched arms form a cross? Can we in our finest moments ever fathom such love and pain?

Sweet Mother, we want to take our place with the shepherds to tell Jesus of our love and gratitude. We want to reach out to the men of all nations just as the Infant reached out to the Wise Men of the East. We want to put aside our prejudice and bigotry and offer the gift of our love to all men.

Obtain for us the grace to see Jesus in the lowly and offer Jesus to the forgotten. Teach us to be holy, so we may give the Father the glory and Jesus the pleasure of making sinners into saints.

THE PRESENTATION

"According to the law of Moses, they took Jesus up to Jerusalem to present Him to the Lord."

— LUKE 2:22

We pray for the mentally challenged: Our Father, ten Hail Marys, Glory Be.

Meditation

Kind Mother, did another Magnificat rise to your lips as you walked up the Temple steps to present Jesus to the Father? What must have been your joy as you gave Jesus to Simeon! Were you expecting this man of God to prophesy the great things this Child would accomplish? Did you think he would shout throughout the Temple precincts, "The Lord has come"?

If you expected great things to be pronounced, was your heart torn by the realization that this Child was a sign of contradiction—destined for the rise and fall of many?

You did not fall beneath this bittersweet experience. The plan of God may not have been to your liking, but you accepted it with all the love of your pure heart.

Obtain for all parents, whose mentally challenged children are specially chosen, like Jesus, to accomplish hidden works for the glory of God, the same courage you manifested in the Temple.

The Child of your womb was destined to be great, but so few recognized that greatness. Give the parents of these special children a deep realization of the power of their suffering. Let their suffering rise to Heaven as sweet-smelling incense for the salvation of souls. Let the beauty of their souls, hidden from the eyes of men in this life, shine like bright stars in the glory of the Father's Kingdom.

Fifth Joyful Mystery

THE FINDING OF THE CHILD JESUS IN THE TEMPLE

"After three days they found Him in the Temple. He was sitting in the midst of the teachers."

— LUKE 2:46

We pray for God's blessings on families and on all the young: Our Father, ten Hail Marys, Glory Be.

Meditation

Kind Mother, we cannot conceive the agony of your pure heart as you looked for your Child for three days. The unspeakable torture of wondering what you had done wrong must have pierced your soul to its very core.

Even the joy of finding Him was mixed with the wonder of why it happened. Today, dear Mother, many families are torn with the grief of those who stray from the right path. Your Son was found in the Temple of the Lord, but our loved ones are often lost on the highways of sin and evil.

Although the place in which we find them is different, the agony is the same.

Obtain for our families a deeper union with the Trinity. Make the father head, the mother heart, and the children members of one another. When the sword of separation in mind, heart, or ideals tears the family apart, grant that the healing balm of love may find them in the temple of God's will, listening to His voice speaking of harmony in the depths of their souls.

The
LUMINOUS
MYSTERIES

Prayed on Thursdays

THE BAPTISM OF JESUS

"Then Jesus appeared: he came from Galilee
to the Jordan to be baptised by John."

— MATTHEW 3:13

We pray for those persecuted for God's sake:
Our Father, ten Hail Marys, Glory Be.

Meditation

Dear Jesus, You were baptized with water, one of the commonest of all substances. Your grace, Your love, Your Spirit—they are all super-abundant and available to all who ask for them. I ask You to open my heart to Your infinite and gracious love.

And yet, dear Jesus, You were baptized by a most uncommon man. John the Baptist was raised in the desert and subsisted on flower blossoms and wild honey. But he was a prophet of truth, whether about You, Your Father, the Scriptures, or himself. The truth imbued his entire life.

The prophets of Your truth, Baptized Lord, have always been scorned. The opinions of men do not matter to You, nor should they matter to us. Strengthen my resolve to follow John the Baptist, not to concern myself with human respect, and to be a light that illuminates not myself but You and You alone.

There is no other. Only Jesus is Savior. Only Jesus is the Messiah. Only Jesus is Lord. Only Jesus prepares a place for us in eternity.

Help me, in my own small ways in my own communities, to prepare the way for You as John the Baptist did two thousand years ago.

Second Luminous Mystery

THE WEDDING AT CANA

"This was the first of Jesus' signs: it was at Cana in Galilee. He revealed his glory, and his disciples believed in him."

— JOHN 2:11

We pray that we may find joy in holiness, and even in suffering: Our Father, ten Hail Marys, Glory Be.

Meditation

At Cana, dear Jesus, Your public ministry began with a quiet miracle at a joyful celebration. This moment was both an echo of the Incarnation and a presaging of the Eucharist and the Passion.

When You turned to Your Mother after she told You that the wine had run out and asked, "What concern is that to you and to me?" You were telling her that she must initiate Your works in the world. Her yes to the Angel Gabriel brought You down to Earth. Her saying, "Do whatever He tells you" to the servants brought forth Your first miracle.

Jesus, help me to trust You as Your Mother trusted You, without question or limitation.

Trust gave her the ability to believe without seeing and to give herself totally to God. Even at this celebration, though, this trust did not come without sorrow. Initiating Your ministry, dear Jesus, meant beginning Your journey to Calvary.

Just as You turned water into wine and You turn wine into blood, turn my broken humanity into a vessel of holiness. May I find joy in that holiness as the revelers at Cana found joy in the wine You gave them, but may I also find joy in persevering through the sufferings that come with trusting You.

Third Luminous Mystery

THE PROCLAMATION OF THE KINGDOM

"After John had been arrested, Jesus went into Galilee. There he proclaimed the gospel from God saying, 'The time is fulfilled, and the kingdom of God is close at hand. Repent, and believe the gospel.'"

— MARK 1:14-15

We pray for the courage to witness to God's truth: Our Father, ten Hail Marys, Glory Be.

Meditation

Dear Jesus, You preached the Good News of repentance and the Kingdom of God even though You knew it would bring ridicule, and ultimately Your Passion.

Now as then, people do not want to hear the truth, and so speaking the truth is frightening. But I must be willing to take any risk for the love of the Kingdom and the Church, and preaching the Good News is essential to my Christian vocation. Help me to overcome my fear, dear Jesus, so that I can be a witness to Your truth and so that through me You can manifest Your presence, Your providence, Your love, and Your mercy.

Only You, Lord, can give me the grace to love when I am hated, to forgive when I am hurt, to be faithful when I fear the darkness, and to have hope when all seems lost.

Build up in me the childlike trust in You that is essential to enter Your Kingdom. I want to do Your will obediently and without hesitation. I want to love You with the unquestioning and wholehearted love of a child for his parents.

I belong to You, my God. Give me the holy zeal to win souls for Your Kingdom.

Fourth Luminous Mystery

THE
TRANSFIGURATION

"There in their presence he was transfigured:
his face shone like the sun and his
clothes became as dazzling as light."

— MATTHEW 17:2

*We pray for the grace to love God and to seek Him even
in darkness: Our Father, ten Hail Marys, Glory Be.*

Meditation

We all want beautiful and joyful moments to last forever. So did the apostles when Jesus was transfigured in blazing light on Mount Tabor.

But I know I must come down from the mountain into the valley, where I can no longer see Your glory as clearly and sometimes feel blind to it altogether. Transfigured Lord, help me to love You and to praise You and to trust You not only in those beautiful moments on the mountaintop but also in the dark times in the valley. Your will is always perfect, both when it is bathes me in light and when it feels as if the darkness will never abate.

When the Father spoke to the apostles, saying, "This is my Son, the Beloved; he enjoys my favour. Listen to him," the apostles cowered in fear. But "when they raised their eyes, they saw no one but Jesus" (Matthew 17:5, 8).

Lord Jesus, whether I am filled with joy or with sorrow, whether my soul feels light or heavy, whether I can feel the warmth of Your love or the coldness of despair, help me to listen and to look to no one except You.

Fifth Luminous Mystery

THE INSTITUTION OF THE EUCHARIST

"And he took bread, and when he had given thanks he broke it and gave it to them, saying, 'This is my body which is given for you. Do this in remembrance of me.'"

— LUKE 22:19

We pray for an increase in reverence for the Eucharist:
Our Father, ten Hail Marys, Glory Be.

Meditation

I live because of the Eucharist. There's no prayer so high; there's no ecstasy so sublime; there's no work so great; there's no suffering so severe; there's nothing to compare with that moment when I and the Trinity — Almighty God through Jesus, Your Son, and the power of Your Spirit — are one. It is the greatest gift You could ever give us.

And yet in the moments before You instituted this most precious gift, Your apostles disputed who was the greatest. Lord God, help me to abandon the preoccupations that seem so important to me as I approach You in the Eucharist, as on Calvary.

You humbled Yourself by becoming man, by permitting Yourself to suffer, and now by masking Your unparalleled glory in the form of a small piece of bread—all so that I can have You inside me.

Lord God, if I truly appreciated the majestic humility of the Eucharist, if I fully grasped the opportunity to participate in Your very nature, it would change my life forever. Strengthen my love and my gratitude for this tremendous gift. Give me the faith to understand that the Eucharist makes everything possible.

The
SORROWFUL
MYSTERIES

Prayed on Tuesdays and Fridays

First Sorrowful Mystery

THE AGONY IN THE GARDEN

"Jesus came with them to Gethsemane
and He began to be saddened
and exceedingly troubled."

— MATTHEW 26:36–37

*We pray for the ability to do God's will and to accept
our crosses: Our Father, ten Hail Marys, Glory Be.*

Meditation

My Jesus, You told Your apostles many times that You looked forward to the final hour of redemption, and yet as You foresaw the sufferings to come, You shuddered with fear and anguish of soul.

You asked the Father to let this chalice pass and You received a refusal. My future looms before me at times, dear Jesus, and I tremble with fear and trepidation. I have implored the Father many times to grant me a favor or to release me from a cross, and His answer has often been no.

Why should I question His wisdom in my regard when He refused His own Son because the good of mankind was at stake? Help me to do the Father's will with Your generosity and to accept a negative reply with Your love.

It is the mental anguish and uncertainty that tears my soul apart, and I often question the Father's love for me.

Your example of resignation, acceptance, and love makes me realize that the Father has my life in His hands and nothing happens to me that is not for my good.

Give me the confidence to ask for what I think I need, the humility to wait for God's will, and the faith to accept a refusal. Let my suffering be redemptive; let my will be one with God's and my life a sacrifice of love.

THE SCOURGING AT THE PILLAR

"Pilate then took Jesus and had Him scourged."

— JOHN 19:1

We pray that we may overcome the weaknesses
that strip us of grace and lead us to unfaithfulness:
Our Father, ten Hail Marys, Glory Be.

Meditation

The pain of this suffering often escapes me, dear Jesus. I forget that this incident was not only painful but humiliating. Each stroke of the whip made You wince with pain, and the gaze of the onlookers made You feel like "a worm and no man" (Ps. 22:6).

Were You thinking of us today as we travel the road of immorality, drugs, alcohol, and unfaithfulness? Did Your divine eyes see the immodesty, perversion, and fornication through the centuries?

Did the thought of how easily men strip themselves of grace for gross pleasure give You the courage to receive one more blow of the lash, one more

wound, and one more sneer? Did the tears of unre-
quited love stream down Your cheeks as You saw so
many laughingly going to perdition?

Surely, my Jesus, this scourging made reparation
for more than the sins of the flesh. Were the welts
that began to bleed suffered for those who tear off
the garments of love and clothe themselves in the
rags of dissension and disobedience?

Was not one lash marked "Rudeness" and another "Hate"? And when the scourging finally
ended, did Your eyes see some blood trickling down
and stepped on as if in derision?

We are sorry, dear Jesus. Cover us all with this
precious blood and heal our many wounds. Let
modesty and purity be our goal and harmony our
motto.

Third Sorrowful Mystery

THE CROWNING WITH THORNS

"And plaiting a crown of thorns they put it upon His head and a reed in His right hand."

— MATTHEW 27:29

We pray that we may overcome pride, worry, and resentments and for an increase in faith: Our Father, ten Hail Marys, Glory Be.

Meditation

My Jesus, I often think my portion of the cross is more than I can bear. It seems to me that I am the recipient of superfluous suffering. My thoughts are empty of reasoning, and my heart is cold. If I remembered that You were crowned with thorns after You were scourged, I would be silent in the presence of divine wisdom.

My pride, stubbornness, and lack of faith tagged each thorn as it pierced Your sacred head. My desire for the glory of this world to the exclusion of spiritual realities tightened the branches around Your head.

My lack of confidence in Your mercy and the lukewarmness of my love braided this instrument of torture into a wreath of unspeakable pain.

Were the tiny thorns that pricked Your head the worries I permit to choke Your Word from my mind? Were the resentments I cherish in my memory the reed that struck Your head? And when the spittle ran down Your face, did my arrogance make You cry?

O Jesus, let me never forget Your love for me and the reparation You offered the Father for my sake. Let my soul magnify the Lord by humility of heart, purity of mind, and a gentle spirit.

THE CARRYING
OF THE CROSS

"And bearing the Cross for Himself, He
went forth to the place called The Skull."

— JOHN 19:17

*We pray that we may obtain courage
in sickness and in sorrow: Our Father,
ten Hail Marys, Glory Be.*

Meditation

You loved me enough, dear Jesus, to take upon Your bleeding shoulders the wood of Your Cross. My love for You is wanting, for I find physical pain difficult to bear, sorrow oppressive, and tragedies cruel.

You have asked that I take whatever the Father permits in my life and follow in Your footsteps, yet I often think the Cross was meant only for You and not for me.

I thought redemption meant freedom from pain, but I know now, as I see this heavy beam on Your back, that Your redeeming Cross gave value to my pain. Your footsteps in the coarse ground cushioned the path for my feet. Your Cross cut a ridge in the earth for my cross to rest in. Your presence cleared the air of hopelessness and showed me the way. Your acceptance took away the curse and bestowed a blessing.

Help me, my Jesus, to carry my cross with joy, keeping my eyes always on the Father's will. Grant that I may not waste time deciding which cross comes from You and which comes from my neighbor. Let me accept all from You, realizing that some crosses correct me, some release me, some prevent me from a life of sin, some are redemptive, and some lead to repentance.

May our cross be one cross, dear Jesus, that together we may glorify the Father and save souls.

Fifth Sorrowful Mystery

THE CRUCIFIXION

"And when they came to the place called
The Skull they crucified Him."

— LUKE 23:33

We pray that we may forgive and love unselfishly:
Our Father, ten Hail Marys, Glory Be.

Meditation

You gave Your life for me when I was a sinner. You loved me, dear Jesus, before I saw the light of day or felt the gentle breeze upon my cheek.

You have suffered and died for me, hounded and pursued me, inspired and drawn me. Your love is totally unselfish, and although I rejoice that I am the recipient of such love, I cannot love unselfishly in return.

You forgave Your enemies and looked away as Your friends deserted You. Is it not strange, dear Jesus, that I still find forgiveness hard and mercy impossible? What is lacking in my life that makes forgiving my neighbor difficult? Is the fact that I cannot forgive myself a factor in my lack of mercy toward others?

Help me, Jesus, to see Your loving gaze as it looked to the Father with abandonment, to the thief with mercy, and to Your Mother with love.

Grant that I may forgive my enemies and abandon myself to the Father's Will. Let me commend my life and my eternity to His care. Let zeal for the salvation of souls make my soul thirst for sacrifice, and let the thought of paradise enlighten my path.

Give me the grace to persevere to the end, and when the journey is over and I have fought the good fight, let the angels sing the last verse of my earthly song: "It is finished" (John 19:30).

The
Glorious
Mysteries

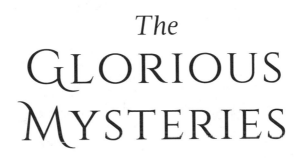

Prayed on Sundays and Wednesdays

First Glorious Mystery

THE RESURRECTION

"He is not here, but has risen. Behold
the place where they laid Him."

— LUKE 24.6, MARK 16.6

*We pray for the grace to bear in mind the
joys to come and to persevere to the end:
Our Father, ten Hail Marys, Glory Be.*

Meditation

Jesus, the joy of Your Resurrection fills my soul with exultation and the realization that my body, too, will rise someday. Like Your five wounds, my suffering will also shine for all to see. The wisdom of the Father will be glorified forever as all men see how His plan and will in my life marked out the glory that would be mine for all eternity.

All the trials, sufferings, heartaches, and disappointments will seem as nothing compared with the glory Your sufferings merited for me. They shall all seem like a dream, and the vision of Your face will fill my soul with exquisite joy.

My soul, reunited to my body, will be perfect as Yours is perfect. No evil tendencies will ever again disturb it, no weakness mar its beauty, no separations grieve my soul, no sickness or tears shatter my peace, no regrets cloud my mind.

My memory, like Yours, dear Jesus, will be filled with good things; my intellect will understand the greatest mysteries; my will, ever united to You, will never again experience the pain of rebellion.

I will love and be loved by everyone, and nothing will be impossible for me. The Father will be ever at my side, and together with You, dear Jesus, I will roam freely in love of the Spirit forever and ever.

Second Glorious Mystery

THE ASCENSION

"And He was taken up into
Heaven and sits at the Right
Hand of God."

— MARK 16:19

*We pray that we may rise above the things of this
world: Our Father, ten Hail Marys, Glory Be.*

Meditation

Dear Jesus, I find the day You ascended to the Father a sad day. It resembles my soul when, after experiencing Your presence, it is plunged into a state of dryness. Like the apostles, I tend to stand still and look up in the hope that I will once again experience the joy of Your presence.

When this happens, my Lord, remind me of the angels' admonition: "Why do you stand here idle looking up to Heaven?" (Acts 1:11).

This dryness of soul is something I must work with and not against. Help me to realize that when I feel Your presence, You are consoling me, but when I do not feel that presence and I continue a life of love and virtue, I am consoling You.

Teach me to prefer consoling You to being consoled, and give me the light to exercise my faith when all seems dark.

I want to rise above the demands of my emotions and have the courage to live in spirit and truth. Grant me the faith that is always aware of the invisible reality, the hope that trusts in Your promises, and the love that seeks not itself.

Third Glorious Mystery

THE DESCENT OF THE HOLY SPIRIT

"And suddenly there came a sound from Spirit Heaven...and there appeared to them parted tongues...and they were filled with the Holy Spirit."

— ACTS 2:2, 3, 4

We pray that we may increase in love and that the Blessed Trinity may dwell in us more fully: Our Father, ten Hail Marys, Glory Be.

Meditation

Mary and the disciples were locked in the Upper Room, praying in a spirit of expectation, and the Spirit of the Lord came in the form of fire over the heads of each one.

At that moment, timid men became strong; fearful men became courageous; ignorant men became enlightened; and simple men became powerful.

Men who lacked the courage to defend their Lord ran out into the streets and proclaimed His Name. Imperfect men, finite and frail, healed the sick, cast out demons, and raised the dead.

These were the men who traveled without money yet made all men rich. They had no place to rest their heads yet ever lived in their Father's house. They were unlearned yet spoke many languages.

They spoke of forgiving enemies and drew men to repentance. They labored and received no pay, yet piled up treasure in the Kingdom.

Holy Spirit, give me an increase of Your gifts and the grace that ensures Your presence in my soul. Give me an awareness of the divine indwelling, a realization of how much the Father loves me, and transform my soul into a perfect image of Jesus.

THE ASSUMPTION

"Hear, O daughter, and see; turn
your ear, for the King shall desire
your beauty. All glorious is the king's
daughter as she enters; her raiment
is threaded with spun gold."

— PSALM 45:10–11, 13–14

*We pray that we may possess a deep awareness of the
glory to come: Our Father, ten Hail Marys, Glory Be.*

Meditation

Mary, my Queen and Mother, I rejoice that your pure body — the Ark of the Covenant before His birth, and a temple of the Lord at His Resurrection — rose from death in anticipation of the general resurrection.

It is a comfort to know that you are in Heaven as my Mother with all the love and concern your dignity demands. You know the dangers of this life, the temptations of the Enemy, and the weaknesses of the flesh. Help me to withstand these dangers until Jesus calls me to Himself.

Teach me, kind Mother, to keep my body pure, my mind undefiled, and my heart detached. Let your Assumption into Heaven give me the assurance and courage to be a Christian in word and deed.

Fill my mind with the knowledge of your Son's life, with compassion for His sufferings, and with zeal for His Kingdom.

Let my life be patterned after His life and my faith and hope be as deep as yours. I want to stand beneath my cross exercising the same stamina with which you stood beneath His. I want my love and zeal to endure any pain and make any sacrifice. Intercede with your Son on my behalf, and teach me to be like Him. Let me rise above the things of this world so my thoughts may be with you in Heaven.

Fifth Glorious Mystery

THE CORONATION

"And a great sign appeared in Heaven:
a woman clothed with the sun, and
the moon under her feet, and upon
her head a crown of twelve stars."

— REVELATION 12:1

*We pray that we may one day be united
with God in His Kingdom: Our Father,
ten Hail Marys, Glory Be.*

Meditation

Dear Mother, the justice of God was not satisfied with reuniting your body and soul so you would be able to imitate Jesus in the Kingdom. Your divine Son, King and Lord, deigned to crown you as Queen of Heaven and Earth.

On earth you were the unknown and unheralded Mother of Jesus. Your humility astonished the angels and confused the proud demons. It is truly just that now your greatness be manifested to all God's children.

Your one desire is to lead us to Jesus, and your one prayer is for our salvation. I am grateful for your care and sorry for my negligence.

Your Coronation gives me assurance that one day I too shall be crowned with glory. God will wipe away every tear from my eyes and bestow on me the light of glory.

Your heart was pierced with seven sorrows during your earthly pilgrimage. Now twelve stars circle your head, and the moon is under your feet. Obtain for me, dear Mother, the grace I need to enter His Kingdom one day and be crowned with the crown of holiness.

THE WAY

of

THE CROSS

OPENING PRAYER

Mary, my Mother, you were the first to live the Way of the Cross. You felt every pain and every humiliation. You were unafraid of the ridicule heaped on you by the crowds. Your eyes were ever on Jesus and His pain. Is that the secret of your miraculous strength? How did your loving heart bear such a burden and such a weight? As you watched Him stumble and fall, were you tortured by the memory of all the yesterdays—His birth, His hidden life, and His ministry?

You were so desirous that everyone love Him. What a heartache it was to see so many hate Him—hate with a diabolical fury. Take my hand as I make this Way of the Cross. Inspire me with the thoughts that will make me realize how much He loves me. Give me light to apply each Station to my daily life and to remember my neighbor's needs in this Way of the Cross.

Obtain for me the grace to understand the mystery, the wisdom, and the divine love as I go from scene to scene. Grant that my heart, like yours, may be pierced through by the sight of Jesus' sorrow and misery and that I may determine never to offend Him again. What a price He paid to cover my sins, to open the gates of heaven for me, and to fill my soul with His Spirit. Sweet Mother, let us travel this way together, and grant that the love in my poor heart may give you some slight consolation.

First Station

JESUS IS CONDEMNED TO DEATH

We adore You, O Christ, and we bless
You, because by Your Holy Cross
You have redeemed the world.

Our Father, Hail Mary, Glory Be

Meditation

My Jesus, the world still has You on trial. It keeps asking who You are and why You make the demands You make. It asks over and over, "If You are God's Son, why do You permit the world to be in the state it is in? Why are You so silent?"

Although the arrogance of the world angers me, I must admit that silently, in the depths of my soul, I too have these questions. Your humility frustrates me and makes me uncomfortable. Your strength before Pilate as You drank deeply from the power of the Father gives me the answer to my question: the Father's Will. The Father permits many sufferings in my life, but they are all for my good. If only I too could be silent in the face of worldly prudence, steadfast in the Faith when all seems lost, calm when accused unjustly, free from the tyranny of human respect, ready to do the Father's will no matter how difficult.

Silent Jesus, give us all the graces we need to stand tall in the face of the ridicule of the world. Give the poor the strength not to succumb to their privation but to be ever aware of their dignity as sons of God. Grant that we might not bend to the crippling disease of worldly glory but be willing to be deprived of all things rather than lose Your friendship. My Jesus, although we are accused daily of being fools, let the vision of Quiet Dignity standing before Monstrous Injustice give us all the courage to be Your followers.

JESUS CARRIES HIS CROSS

We adore You, O Christ, and we bless
You, because by Your Holy Cross
You have redeemed the world.

Our Father, Hail Mary, Glory Be

Meditation

How could any human impose such a burden on Your torn and bleeding body, Lord Jesus? Each movement of the Cross drove the thorns deeper into Your head. How did You keep the hatred from welling up in Your heart? How did the injustice of it all not ruffle Your peace? The Father's will was hard on You. Why do I complain when it is hard on me?

I see injustice and am frustrated, and when my plans to alleviate it seem futile, I despair. When I see those burdened with poverty suffer ever more, and cross is added to cross, my heart is far from serene. I utterly fail to see the dignity of the cross as it is carried with love. I would so much rather be without it.

My worldly concept is that suffering, like food, should be shared equally. How ridiculous I am, dear Lord. Just as we do not all need the same amount of material food, neither do we need the same amount of spiritual food, and that is what the cross is in my life, isn't it—spiritual food proportional to my needs.

My Jesus, You embraced Your Cross with great love. You knew its power; You saw the Father's will. Most of the crosses I have are of my own making—they are there because I refuse to cheerfully carry the simple one You have given me. Let me never forget that the injustice of the world may be accomplishing the justice of God in my soul.

Third Station

JESUS FALLS THE FIRST TIME

We adore You, O Christ, and we bless
You, because by Your Holy Cross
You have redeemed the world.

Our Father, Hail Mary, Glory Be

Meditation

My Jesus, it seems to me that, as God, You would have carried Your Cross without faltering, but You did not. You fell beneath its weight to show me You understand when I fall. Is it pride that makes me want to shine even in pain? You were not ashamed to fall — to admit the Cross was heavy. There are those whom my pride will not tolerate, as I want everyone to be strong, yet I am weak. I am ashamed to admit failure in anything.

If the Father permits failure in my life, just as He permitted You to fall, then I must know that in that failure there is good that my mind will never comprehend. I must not concentrate on the eyes of others as they rest upon me in my falls. Rather, I must reach up to touch that invisible hand and drink in that invisible strength ever at my side.

Weak Jesus, help all men who try so hard to be good but whose nature is constantly opposed to their walking straight and tall down the narrow road of life. Raise their heads to see the glory that is to come rather than the misery of the present moment.

Your love for me gave You strength to rise from Your fall. Look on all those whom the world considers unprofitable servants, and give them the courage to be more concerned as to how they stand before You rather than their fellowmen.

Fourth Station

JESUS MEETS HIS AFFLICTED MOTHER

We adore You, O Christ, and we bless
You, because by Your Holy Cross
You have redeemed the world.

❧

Our Father, Hail Mary, Glory Be

Meditation

My Jesus, it was a great sorrow to realize that Your pain caused Mary so much grief. As Redeemer, You wanted her to share in Your pain for mankind. When You glanced at each other in unutterable suffering, what gave You both the courage to carry on without the least alleviation—without anger at such injustice?

It seems as if You desired to suffer every possible pain to give me an example of how to suffer when my time comes. What a humiliation for You when Your Mother saw You in such a pitiable state—weak, helpless, at the mercy of sinful men—holiness exposed to evil in all hideousness.

Did every moment of that short encounter seem like an eternity? As I see so much suffering in the world, there are times I think it is all hopeless. There is an element of lethargy in my prayers for mankind that says, "I'll pray, but what good will it do? The sick grow sicker, and the hungry starve." I think of that glance between You and Mary — the glance that said, "Let us give this misery to the Father for the salvation of souls. The Father's power takes our pain and frustration and renews souls, saves them for a new life — a life of eternal joy, eternal happiness. It is worth it all." Give perseverance to the sick so they can carry the cross of frustration and agony with love and resignation for the salvation of others.

SIMON HELPS JESUS CARRY HIS CROSS

We adore You, O Christ, and we bless
You, because by Your Holy Cross
You have redeemed the world.

Our Father, Hail Mary, Glory Be

Meditation

My Jesus, Your tormentors enlisted Simon of Cyrene to help You carry Your Cross. Your humility is beyond my comprehension. Your power upheld the whole universe, yet You permit one of Your creatures to help You carry a cross. I imagine Simon was reluctant to take part in Your shame. He had no idea that all who watched and jeered at him would pass into oblivion while his name would go down in history and eternity as the one who helped his God in need. Is it not so with me, dear Jesus? Even when I reluctantly carry my cross as Simon did, it benefits my soul.

If I keep my eyes on You and watch how You suffered, I will be able to bear my cross with greater fortitude. Were You trying to tell all those who suffer from prejudice to have courage? Was Simon a symbol of all those who are hated because of race, color, or creed?

As he took that beam upon his shoulders, Simon wondered why he was chosen for such a heavy burden, and now he knows. Help me, Jesus, to trust Your loving providence as You permit suffering to weave itself in and out of my life. Make me understand that You looked at it and held it fondly before You passed it on to me. You watch me and give me strength just as You did Simon. When I enter Your Kingdom, I shall know, as he knows, what marvels Your Cross has wrought in my soul.

Veronica Wipes the Face of Jesus

We adore You, O Christ, and we bless
You, because by Your Holy Cross
You have redeemed the world.

Our Father, Hail Mary, Glory Be

Meditation

My Jesus, where were all the hundreds of peoples whose bodies and souls You had healed? Where were they when You needed someone to give You the least sign of comfort? Ingratitude must have borne down on Your heart and made the Cross nearly impossible to carry. There are times I too feel all my efforts for Your Kingdom are futile and end in nothingness. Did Your eyes roam through the crowd for the comfort of just one individual, one sign of pity, one sign of grief?

My heart thrills with a sad joy when I think of one woman, breaking away from fear and human respect and offering You her thin veil to wipe Your bleeding face. Your loving heart, ever watching for the least sign of love, imprinted the image of Your torn face upon it! How can You forget Yourself so completely and reward such a small act of kindness?

I must admit, I have been among those who were afraid to know You rather than like Veronica. She did not care if the whole world knew she loved You. Heartbroken Jesus, give me that quality of soul so necessary to witness to and spread Your Word—to tell all people of Your love for them. Send many into Your vineyard so the people of all nations may receive the Good News. Imprint Your divine image upon my soul, and let the thin veil of my human nature bear a perfect resemblance to Your loving Spirit.

Seventh Station

JESUS FALLS THE SECOND TIME

We adore You, O Christ, and we bless
You, because by Your Holy Cross
You have redeemed the world.

Our Father, Hail Mary, Glory Be

Meditation

My Jesus, one of the beautiful qualities the people admired in You was Your strength in time of ridicule — Your ability to rise above the occasion. But now You fall a second time — apparently conquered by the pain of the Cross. People who judge You by appearances made a terrible mistake. What looked like weakness was unparalleled strength!

I often judge by the appearance, and how wrong I am most of the time. The world judges entirely by this fraudulent method of discerning. It looks down on those who apparently have given their best and are now in need. It judges the poor as failures, the sick as useless, and the aged as a burden. How wrong that kind of judgment is in the light of Your second fall! Your greatest moment was Your weakest one. Your greatest triumph was in failure. Your greatest act of love was in desolation. Your greatest show of power was in that utter lack of strength that threw You to the ground.

Weak and powerful Jesus, give me the grace to see beyond what is visible and be more aware of Your wisdom in the midst of weakness. Give the aged, the sick, the handicapped, the mentally impaired, the deaf, and the blind the fruit of joy so they may ever be aware of the Father's gift and the vast difference between what the world sees and what the Father sees, so that they may glory in their weakness so the power of God may be manifest.

JESUS SPEAKS TO THE HOLY WOMEN

We adore You, O Christ, and we bless
You, because by Your Holy Cross
You have redeemed the world.

Our Father, Hail Mary, Glory Be

Meditation

My Jesus, I am amazed at Your compassion for others in Your time of need. When I suffer, I have a tendency to think only of myself, but You forgot Yourself completely. When You saw the holy women weeping over Your torments, You consoled them and taught them to look deeper into Your Passion. You wanted them to understand that the real evil to cry over was the rejection You suffered from the Chosen People — a people set apart from every other nation, who refused to accept God's Son.

The act of redemption would go on, and no one would ever be able to take away Your dignity as the

Son of God, but the evil, greed, jealousy, and ambition in the hearts of those who should have recognized You was the issue to grieve over. To be so close to God-made-man and miss Him completely was the real crime.

My Jesus, I fear I do the same when I strain out gnats and then swallow camels, when I take out the splinter in my brother's eye and forget the beam in my own. Faith is such a gift. It is such a sublime grace to possess Your Spirit. Why haven't I advanced in holiness of life? I miss the many disguises You take upon Yourself and see only people, circumstances, and human events, not the loving hand of the Father guiding all things. Help all those who are discouraged, sick, lonely, and elderly to recognize Your presence in their midst.

Ninth Station

JESUS FALLS THE THIRD TIME

We adore You, O Christ, and we bless
You, because by Your Holy Cross
You have redeemed the world.

Our Father, Hail Mary, Glory Be

Meditation

My Jesus, even with the help of Simon, You fell a third time. Were You telling me that there may be times in my life when I will fall again and again, despite the help of friends and loved ones? There are times when the crosses You permit in my life are more than I can bear. It is as if all the sufferings of a lifetime are suddenly compressed into the present moment, and it is more than I can stand.

Although it grieves my heart to see You so weak and helpless, it is a comfort to my soul to know that You understand my sufferings from Your experience. Your love for me made You want to experience every kind of pain just so I could have someone to look to for example and courage.

When I cry out from the depths of my soul, "This suffering is more than I can bear," do You whisper, "Yes, I understand"? When I am discouraged after many falls, do You say in my innermost being, "Keep going. I know how hard it is to rise"?

There are many people who are sorely tried in body and soul with alcohol and drug weaknesses, who try and try and fall again and again. Through the humiliation of this third fall, give them the courage and perseverance to take up their cross and follow You.

JESUS IS STRIPPED OF HIS GARMENTS

We adore You, O Christ, and we bless
You, because by Your Holy Cross
You have redeemed the world.

Our Father, Hail Mary, Glory Be

Meditation

It seems that every step to Calvary brought You fresh humiliation, my Jesus. How Your sensitive nature recoiled at being stripped before a crowd of people. You desired to leave this life as You entered it—completely detached from all the comforts of this world. You want me to know without a doubt that You loved me with an unselfish love. Your love for me caused You nothing but pain and sorrow. You gave everything and received nothing in return. Why do I find it so hard to be detached?

In Your loving mind, dear Jesus, did You look up to the Father as You stood there on that windy hill, shivering from cold and shame and trembling from fear, and ask Him to have mercy on those who would violate their purity and make love a mockery? Did You ask forgiveness for those whose greed would make them lie, cheat, and steal for a few pieces of cold silver?

Forgive us all, dear Jesus. Look on the world with pity, for mankind has lost its way, and the principles of this world make lust a fun game and luxury a necessity. Detachment has become merely another hardship of the poor and obedience the fault of the weak. Have mercy on us and grant the people of this day the courage to see and know themselves and the light to change.

Eleventh Station

JESUS IS NAILED TO THE CROSS

We adore You, O Christ, and we bless
You, because by Your Holy Cross
You have redeemed the world.

Our Father, Hail Mary, Glory Be

Meditation

It is hard to imagine a God being nailed to a cross by His own creatures. It is even more difficult for my mind to understand a love that permitted such a thing to happen! As those men drove heavy nails into Your hands and feet, dear Jesus, did You offer the pain as reparation for some particular human weakness and sin? Was the nail in Your right hand for those who spend their lives in dissipation and boredom?

Was the nail in Your left and in reparation for all consecrated souls who live lukewarm lives? Were You stretching out Your arms to show us how much You love us? As the feet that walked the hot, dusty roads were nailed fast, did they cramp up in a deadly grip of pain to make reparation for all those who so nimbly run the broad road of sin and self-indulgence?

It seems, dear Jesus, that Your love has held You bound hand and foot as Your heart pleads for a return of love. You seem to shout from the top of the hill, "I love you. Come to me. See, I am held fast. I cannot hurt you. Only you can hurt me." How very hard is the heart that can see such love and turn away. Is it not true that I, too, have turned away when I did not accept the Father's will with love? Teach me to keep my arms ever open to love, to forgive, and to render service—willing to be hurt rather than to hurt, satisfied to love and not be loved in return.

Twelfth Station

JESUS DIES ON THE CROSS

We adore You, O Christ, and we bless
You, because by Your Holy Cross
You have redeemed the world.

Our Father, Hail Mary, Glory Be

Meditation

God is dead! No wonder the earth quaked, the sun hid itself, the dead rose, and Mary stood by in horror. Your human body gave up its soul in death, but Your divinity, dear Jesus, continued to manifest its power. All creation rebelled as the Word-made-flesh departed from this world. Man alone was too proud to see and too stubborn to acknowledge truth.

Redemption was accomplished! Man would never have an excuse to forget how much You loved him. The thief on Your right saw something he could not explain: he saw a man on a tree and knew He was God. His need made him see his own guilt and Your innocence. The promise of eternal life made the remaining hours of his torture endurable.

A common thief responded to Your love with deep faith, hope, and love. He saw more than his eyes envisioned; he felt a presence he could not explain and would not argue with. He was in need and accepted the way God deigned to help him.

Forgive our pride, dear Jesus, as we spend hours speculating, days arguing, and often a lifetime in rejecting Your death, which is a sublime mystery. Have pity on those whose intelligence leads them to pride because they never feel the need to reach out to the Man of Sorrows for consolation.

JESUS IS TAKEN DOWN FROM THE CROSS

We adore You, O Christ, and we bless
You, because by Your Holy Cross
You have redeemed the world.

Our Father, Hail Mary, Glory Be

Meditation

My Jesus, it was with deep grief that Mary finally took You into her arms and saw all the wounds sin had inflicted on You. Mary Magdalene looked on Your dead body with horror. Nicodemus, the man so full of human respect, who came to You by night, suddenly received the courage to help Joseph take You down from the Cross. You are once more surrounded by only a few followers. When loneliness and failure cross my path, let me think of this lonely moment and this total failure—failure in the eyes of men. How wrong they were—how mistaken their concept of success! The greatest act of love was given in desolation and the most successful mission accomplished and finished when all seemed lost. Is this not true in my life, dear Jesus? I judge my failures harshly. I demand perfection instead of holiness. My idea of success is for all to end well—according to my liking.

Give to all men the grace to see that doing Your will is more important than success. If failure is permitted for my greater good, then teach me how to use it to my advantage. Let me say, as You once said, that to do the will of the Father is my food. Let not the standards of this world take possession of me or destroy the good You have set for me—to be holy and to accomplish the Father's will with great love. Let me accept praise or blame, success or failure with equal serenity.

JESUS IS LAID IN THE SEPULCHER

We adore You, O Christ, and we bless
You, because by Your Holy Cross
You have redeemed the world.

Our Father, Hail Mary, Glory Be

Meditation

My Jesus, You were laid to rest in a stranger's tomb. You were born with nothing of this world's goods, and You died detached from everything. When You came into the world, men slept and angels sang, and now as You leave it, creation is silent and only a few weep. Both events were clothed in obscurity. The majority of men live in such a way. Most of us live and die knowing and known by only a few. Were You trying to tell us, dear Jesus, how very important our lives are just because we are accomplishing the Father's will? Will we ever learn the lesson of humility that makes us content with who we are, where we are, and what we are?

Will our faith ever be strong enough to see power in weakness and good in the sufferings of our lives? Will our hope be trusting enough to rely on Your providence even when we have nowhere to lay our head? Will our love ever be strong enough not to take scandal in the Cross?

My Jesus, hide my soul in Your heart as You lie in the sepulcher alone. Let my heart be as a fire to keep You warm. Let my desire to know and love You be like a torch to light up the darkness. Let my soul sing softly a hymn of repentant love as the hours pass and Your Resurrection is at hand. Let me rejoice, dear Jesus, with all the angels in a hymn of praise and thanksgiving for so great a love, so great a God, so great a day!

CLOSING PRAYER

My Jesus, I have traveled Your Way of the Cross. It seems so real, and I feel so ashamed. I complain of my sufferings and find obedience to the Father's will difficult, with my mind bogged down by the poverty, sickness, starvation, greed, and hatred in the world.

There are many innocent people who suffer so unjustly. There are those born with physical and mental defects. Do we understand that You continue to carry Your Cross in the minds and bodies of each person?

Help me to see the Father's will in every incident of my daily life. This is what You did: You saw the Father's will in Your persecutors, Your enemies, and Your pain. You saw a beauty in the Cross and embraced it as a desired treasure.

My worldly mind is dulled by injustice and suffering, and I lose sight of the glory that is to come. Help me to trust the Father and to realize that there is something great behind the most insignificant suffering. There is Someone lifting my cross to fit my shoulders; there is Divine Wisdom in all the petty annoyances that irk my soul every day.

Teach me the lessons contained in my cross, the wisdom of its necessity, the beauty of its variety, and the fortitude that accompanies even the smallest cross. Mary, my Mother, obtain for me the grace to be Jesus to my neighbor and to see my neighbor in Jesus.

MOTHER
ANGELICA'S
CONVERSATION

with

GOD

Humility

I stand before You, Lord God, a sinner. In all the realms of Your creation, no one is more undeserving of Your love than I.... This is why I dare approach Your presence.... Your power is at its best in weakness. Your love is more gratuitous to the ungrateful and Your mercy more sublime to the undeserving.

Hope

My God, You are my anchor on a stormy sea, my serenity on a windy night, my hope when all else fails. Your presence surrounds me like a protective shield and when the arrows of my selfishness pierce through, Your loving arms extend themselves to reach out and grasp my wandering soul.

Detachment

It has taken me so long to surrender to Your love and providence … to release my tensions to Your serenity, my fears to Your omnipotence, and my lukewarmness to Your love. I hold on to these weaknesses as though they were treasures. My soul cries out for freedom, and the very will that reaches for deliverance from tyranny keeps my soul a prisoner to myself.

Longing

I do not ask for the riches that perish or the fame that fades away like a morning mist. I beg only for the freedom of a child of God with one goal, one love, one desire: to please You. My heart longs for You, O God. My soul cries out to You. Living without You is like a desert devoid of life and beauty. Can it be that the dry sand and the scorching heat sear my soul and cleanse it of all those frailties that make me so unlike You? Must I roam through life seeking and finding You only to lose You again?

Desire

Does the torture of losing You and the ecstasy of finding You shape and reshape my soul into Your image? Does the reaching out to touch Your hand and the falling back by missing it exercise my will?

Do You hide when I almost catch a glimpse of You, so I will seek more ardently?

Love

What secret must I find that will enable me to love You alone and above all things, to see You in my neighbor, in the sufferings of my life and in the joys that are sprinkled here and there to give me a peek into Heaven?

Desire

Jesus, although crowds surround me, my soul is alone, and the silence frightens me. To hear noise outside and feel silence inside gives me the feeling of living in two worlds at the same time. One world clamors for my attention and another for my love. O God, I choose Your world—I choose to roam the limitless realms of Your love, always seeing new beauty, always hearing the music of Your merciful forgiveness.

Humility

My mind, O God, struggles with the mystery of Your eternity and trinity. It is so humiliating to reach a point that I cannot pass—the point at which a created mind realizes its capacity is too small to encompass the Infinite. Then it is, O God, that my soul sees itself as it really is—created and limited. It becomes content to wait until Your goodness deigns to raise it, through faith, to the unreachable stars of mystery.

Detachment

You never take Your eyes from me, and yet my eyes wander through the world looking for a place to rest. Why can't I love You as You love me? Why do I seek what is finite when I can possess the Infinite? My fickleness must astound the angels, who see how passing are the things I cling to.

Faith

O Spirit of the Lord, faith propels my mind and soul to those realms of mystery unattainable by my own efforts. What impulse of love made You raise my poor soul above itself? Is my weakness a challenge to Your mercy as Lord of all? Did You as Trinity roam the earth looking for some weak creature on whom You could bestow the treasure of treasures—grace? Your compassionate love, gracious Father, tugs at my selfishness to strip me of the rags I cling to, in order to clothe me in the beautiful garments of holiness.

Patience

Every day, my Jesus, I learn by some situation or experience of my great need for You. When I try to be patient on my own, my patience is forced and short-lived. It is obvious to everyone that I am desperately trying to be patient. When I raise my mind and heart to You, dear Jesus, and see You so serenely patient, my soul drinks in that spirit of patience like a cool breeze on a humid night. Your patience penetrates my being, and only then am

I truly patient. It takes so long to learn that I can bear fruit only in You.

How very much You love me! Love is proven by sacrifice, and You have proven Your love for me. This realization makes me feel small, for I am forced to admit that my love for You is very little. I run from sacrifice and am afraid of pain. Death at times seems like a dark tunnel to be traveled, and the future seems bleak. When I compare my attitude with Yours, I realize that in myself I have nothing to offer You. The only claim I have is Your love for me. When I think of that love, I feel a sudden surge of courage to face the future. Even death becomes merely the beautiful moment when the One who loves and the one who is loved meet face-to-face.

Courage

Lord Father, life is always easier when I keep close to You. Sometimes I wonder why it is so hard to keep my soul united to the only source of happiness. It would seem that I should be drawn to You like a piece of iron to a magnet, and yet my own will and frailties form a barrier that keeps my soul separated from You. The very thing I want to be, I am not. I run away from the pruning I need in order to be like You. My life is such a contradiction. My soul yearns for holiness and then runs from the mortification necessary to attain it. I shall have to depend on You, dear Jesus, to lift my poor soul out of its weakness and clothe it with the courage and strength of Your Holy Spirit.

Then You will bear fruit in me — fruit pleasing to the Father.

Self-Knowledge

Master, no one really sees himself or his actions as others see them. Perhaps, looking into the motives that I attribute to others may give me a glimpse into my own soul. I will not like what I see there but let Your Spirit make the picture really clear so with Your help I may change and begin to think and act like Jesus.

Presence of God

Lord Trinity, I want to be more aware of Your divine presence in my soul. I know your life with me is often lonely. I flit from one unimportant thing to another, and then when my heart becomes empty and lonely, I seek You. Why do I run to You only after all else fails? You are the only light that guides my path, the only love that is faithful, the only strength in time of weakness. Be patient with me, Lord, and grant that someday my mind will have no thought that is not pleasing to You and my heart possess no love stronger than its love for You.

Companionship

There are times, my Jesus, when I like to imagine Your face and picture how You walked down dusty roads. I like to think You are standing beside me, watching all I do with great love and understanding. Then I realize that once more I have brought

You down to my size, encompassed Your beauty in the narrow realms of my imagery, and constrained You in a tiny space beside me. My Lord, this is the only way my poor human nature can arrive at some concept of You. Grant, dear Jesus, that when my imagination pictures You, I never lose sight of the truth that Your real beauty is beyond my wildest dreams. Your presence is much closer than at my side.

Forgiveness

Lord Father, I enter into Your compassionate Spirit and try to drink deeply of Your merciful love. My memory smarts with the remembrance of past offenses, and my soul is pained by the anger of yesterdays—days in the past that bring tears and sadness. Every time I think they are gone, they return with renewed vigor, and I realize I have not grown in compassion and forgiveness. I put my memory into Your compassionate mercy, and I ask You to cover its wounds with the healing balm of Your mercy. Let my soul sink deep into that fathomless ocean of mercy and return to me renewed, healed, and refreshed with love for everyone and malice toward none.

Anger

Lord Jesus, I feel angry today—angry at the world because it is greedy, angry at people because they are selfish, and angry at myself because I am not what I should be. Quiet my soul with Your gentleness, and let that peaceful attitude permeate my soul with the compassionate understanding I need to be kind and objective.

Time

Life is so short, my Lord. I look at all my yesterdays, and they seem so hazy, while all my tomorrows are uncertain. The only time I really possess is this tiny moment, and it passes so quickly. Why does time weigh so heavily in my life? It is a most precious gift from Your hands, and I should look at it as I would a treasure. It provides the opportunity for me to know You better and love You more, to become like Jesus and be filled with Your own Spirit, to increase in holiness and to make reparation for my sins. Thank You, my Lord, for time. Please grant me more time to love You and

tell You how very sorry I am for ever having of-
fended You.

Suffering

I feel sick today, dear Jesus. My head throbs, and
my body is so weak that it is an effort even to talk
to You. I try to think of Your poor head when it
was crowned with thorns, and I marvel at Your
fortitude. I think of how very weak You must have
been when You took the Cross upon Your shoulders. I marvel at Your love. Love was the driving
power that made You strong when You were weak.
If I could realize Your love was for *me*. Well then,
I will do the same for You. It is strange, dear Jesus,
that as soon as I think of Your pain, mine seems
slight.

To You, dear Jesus, life was a mission and You were the Father's message to the world: You were to save it; You were to open the gates of Heaven to poor human beings. Did You ever get tired of Your mission, especially when so many did not listen? Were You ever sorry You came? I know these are silly questions. Your love was so burning that each moment, even the most painful, was sweet and light. Grant that I may love like You and never count the cost.

Eternity

O God, I wish I could look upon the whole world from the viewpoint of Your eternity. How differently I would see everything. Things would look very small, and people would live and die in such a short span of time. From that vantage point, centuries would pass like a few days. The tallest mountain would be as a speck of dust and all the oceans as drops of water. I would see nations and kingdoms come and go. Many small people would start big wars and destroy other people; then, like a puff of smoke, they would be gone and all their ambitions turned to nothing. Truly, looking down from such a height would change my goals and desires. Although I must live in a world that looks very big and feels very permanent, grant that I may never lose sight of the truth that in reality it is very small and very transitory. You alone are changeless, and You alone are Great. You alone, Lord God, are worthy of praise and honor and glory.

Discouragement

O God, my mind whirls around in confusion, and my soul seems destitute of all consolation. It is as if all the world and all my life were telescoped into one moment and I carry the burden of it all. I cannot see any future except tomorrow being another today. All my yesterdays crowd around me, some accusing and some filled with regret. It is like a prison with a thousand voices shouting for attention. Divine Jailor, You have the key to release my soul from the prison of discouragement. Unlock the doors, and let me roam freely into the regions of Your love. Deliver me from the tyranny of my own will. Surely You take no pleasure in my soul disquieted within me, for then I am wrapped in myself. Do I hear You whisper, "Unlock the door for the key is within; I wait ready to enter and comfort you"?

Wonder and Awe

My Jesus, I praise Your beauty! Everything You created bears the stamp of beauty and the marvel of it all is its variety. What made You decide the color of a rose and the height of a mountain, the way a stream gently winds around a bend and then ends up in a roaring waterfall? When man first appeared on earth and said, "I love You, God," did Your heart thrill? And when he said, "I will not serve," did You cry? I know I shall have to wait until we meet for the answers to these mysteries, but it thrills my heart that a God so great can be asked such puzzling questions.

Healing of Memory

Lord Father, heal my memory. It is like a store-house out of which come old things and new, good things and bad. It is strange, but sometimes an event that happened years ago suddenly looms up and the hurt returns, and with it anger and resentment. Jesus told us to be as compassionate and merciful as You are. I find this very hard, and yet why should I? Have I not been the recipient of Your mercy and forgiveness? Is it not a greater thing for me to offend God than for a fellow creature to offend me? You forgive and forget so completely and so graciously. Let me bury all my unpleasant memories in Your ocean of mercy and drown them forever in those peaceful waters. May the phantoms of yesterday never take up residence in today and destroy my tomorrow. Give me hope, Lord Father, to trust in Your forgiveness, and let me always give my neighbor the benefit of the doubt so I may forgive him from my heart. Let me never presume upon Your mercy but ever have confidence in Your compassionate heart. Let hope raise my memory above the mud within it and live in the clear water of Your grace.

Search for God

Lord God, my soul reaches out to You in the midst of a void that nothing can fill. My soul, like a butterfly, flits from one thing to another seeking rest and finding none. It is only in You that my weary soul finds fulfillment. I go through life seeking You, and when I think I have found You, the darkest night descends and You are gone. It is then, when the new dawn slowly breaks through, that I once more find You. As I go through the day seeking You, I find You in unexpected places. My life is truly a game of lost and found. Let my seeking be a love song from a soul bereft of the talent to tell You of its love. Let my fumbling ways be a poem of desire that tells You I love You. Let my weaknesses and failures be like the plaintive cry of a wounded bird that cannot fly to its nest alone. Let my nothingness be lost in Your omnipotence so I may never be separated from You.

> *"You will weep no more. He will be gracious to you when He hears your cry; when He hears He will answer." (Isaiah 30:19)*

Biographical Note

Mother Mary Angelica of the Annunciation was born Rita Antoinette Rizzo on April 20, 1923, in Canton, Ohio.

After a difficult childhood, a healing of her recurring stomach ailment led the young Rita on a process of discernment that ended with her entering the Poor Clares of Perpetual Adoration in Cleveland. Thirteen years later, in 1956, Sister Angelica promised the Lord as she awaited spinal surgery that, if He would permit her to walk again, she would build Him a monastery in the South.

In Irondale, Alabama, Mother Angelica's vision took form. Her distinctive approach to teaching the Faith led to parish talks, then pamphlets and books, then radio and television opportunities. By 1980 the Nuns had converted a garage at the monastery into a rudimentary television studio. EWTN was born.

Mother Angelica has been a constant presence on television in the United States and around the world for more than thirty-five years. Innumerable conversions to the Catholic Faith have been attributed to her unique gift for presenting the gospel: joyful but resolute, calming but bracing.

In 1999 Mother Angelica moved to the second monastery she built: Our Lady of the Angels in Hanceville, Alabama. The Nuns spend their days in prayer and in adoration of Our Lord in the Most Blessed Sacrament.